Meeting with Success

Tips and Techniques for Great Meetings

Meeting with Success

Tips and Techniques for Great Meetings

Ida Shessel

Second Edition

Oshawa, Ontario

Meeting with Success:
Tips and Techniques for Great Meetings
by Ida Shessel

Acquisitions Editor: Kevin Aguanno
Typesetting: Tak Keung Sin
Cover Design: Cheung Hoi

Published by:
Multi-Media Publications Inc.
Box 58043, Rosslynn RPO, Oshawa, Ontario, Canada, L1J 8L6.

http://www.mmpubs.com/

All rights reserved. No part of this book may be reproduced or transmitted in any form or by any means, electronic or mechanical, including photocopying, recording or by any information storage and retrieval system, without written permission from the author, except for the inclusion of brief quotations in a review.

Copyright © 2007 by Multi-Media Publications Inc.

ISBN-13 (Adobe PDF ebook):   9781897326114
ISBN-13 (Microsoft LIT ebook):   9781897326122
ISBN-13 (Mobipocket PRC ebook):   9781897326138
ISBN-13 (Palm PDB ebook):   9781897326145
ISBN-13 (Trade Paperback):   9781897326152

Published in Canada.

Formerly published in 2002 by Let Us Facilitate under ISBN 0-9731784-1-8.

Library and Archives Canada Cataloguing in Publication

Shessel, Ida
    Meeting with success: tips and techniques for great meetings / Ida Shessel. -- 2nd ed.

Includes bibliographical references.
Also available in electronic format.
ISBN 978-1-897326-15-2

1. Meetings. I. Title.

HF5734.5.S47 2007   658.4'56   C2006-906726-0

Table of Contents

Making Meetings Matter 7

What's the Problem with Our Meetings? 9

What's the P.O.I.N.T? 11

"P" is for Purpose 13
    If At First You Don't Want To Meet... Don't 14
    Determining The Type Of Meeting 16
    Establishing the Purpose 17

"O" is for Organization 19
    The Time Is Now 20
    Length Matters: Keeping It Short 21
    Your New Best Friend: The Agenda 22
    The Elements Of Your Agenda 22
    Getting The Word Out 24
    The Ground Rules 26
    Keeping Records 28

"I" is for Involvement 31
    Mr. Jones Requests The Honor Of Your
        Presence 31
    Who Are The People In Your Neighborhood? ... 32
    Conflict & Resolution 35
    Encouraging Involvement 35
    Creativity Tools For Idea Generation 36
    Now Think Creatively 38

Meeting with Success

    Decision-Making & Problem-Solving
        Techniques 42
    Analysis – Assessing the Idea Generating
        Efforts 48

"N" is for Navigation 51

"T" is for Tasks 57
    Facilitator 57
    Participants 59
    Time Keeper 60
    Minute Taker 61

Into Action 63

Bibliography 65

About the Author 67

Other Books by Ida Shessel 69

CHAPTER ONE

Making Meetings Matter

Meetings! They may be the heart and soul of business operations but to many of us, they're often nothing more than a royal pain in the rear.

Statistics abound about how much time we spend in meetings – anywhere from 8 to 25 hours per week, depending upon our jobs and status. Of course, it feels even longer than that when we also consider the amount of time we spend preparing for *and* getting to and from meetings.

Perhaps the greatest problem is not the amount of time that goes into the meetings but the fact that most of us feel we are not communicating or accomplishing enough during these sessions. The bottom line is that we're spending an awful lot of time engaged in an activity we don't generally consider effective or productive.

Meeting with Success

Studies on the subject have yielded evidence that ineffective meetings cost us nearly $100 million annually when lost revenue, lack of productivity, and salaries of attendees are taken into account. That's a waste of *far* more than just time.

Does this mean we should just stop having meetings? Before you get too excited, the answer is "no." The problem, you see, isn't actually the meetings themselves – but *how* we meet. Our meetings have deteriorated into inconvenient, ineffective, productivity-zapping wastes of time. We've strayed far from the intended effectiveness of this fundamental business tool.

And yet, we continue to have meetings.

In the following chapters, you'll find all the knowledge and tools you need to make sure every meeting you have is focused and productive. So, whether you're a facilitator, an attendee, or a presenter, prepare to rethink your approach to meetings as we examine:

- Common problems and complaints that spell meeting disaster.
- The P.O.I.N.T. every meeting planner should know · Essential tools, rules, and techniques for a successful meeting.
- What you need to know about people and players.
- Fool-proof methods to motivate and inspire.

So let's get started. Let's learn how to revolutionize your approach to meetings.

CHAPTER TWO

What's the Problem with Our Meetings?

It's a good question – and a great starting point for the journey we're about to take. What *is* the problem with today's meetings? Chances are you already know the answer – or answers.

Do any of these sound familiar?

- They never start on time.
- Whoever is supposed to be running the show clearly has no idea what he or she is doing.
- No one sticks to the topic at hand.
- Half the people don't bother to show up.
- The sales manager's cell phone rings incessantly.

Meeting with Success

- That one guy from accounting is always shooting down everyone else's ideas.
- The room is claustrophobic and the good muffins are gone by the time you get there.
- The same four people are doing all the talking.
- The presenter is droning on despite the fact that half the room has lost consciousness and the other half is "out to lunch".
- No one seems to know why they're there in the first place and even if they did…
- …they've *all* got somewhere far more important to be.

And the list goes on…Fortunately, getting your meetings back on track is really quite simple.

The same skills that you rely on to keep the rest of your business efforts in tip-top shape – focus, organization, and concentration – are all that it takes to turn your organization's meetings into productive gatherings.

So with that in mind, we can now get straight to the **P.O.I.N.T.**…..

CHAPTER THREE

What's the P.O.I.N.T?

You've certainly spent enough time in meetings asking yourself, "What's the point to all of this?" Little did you know that you'd hit the nail on the head – establishing the P.O.I.N.T. of your meeting is the secret to your success.

When we talk about the P.O.I.N.T. of your meeting, we aren't just talking about the purpose of the gathering – although that's a key factor. We're talking about a five-letter, handy-dandy acronym to help you remember the crucial elements of having focused, productive meetings.

Purpose

Organization

Involvement

Navigation

Tasks

Meeting with Success

So dive right into the following sections, each of which will walk you through these five essential elements for getting your meetings on track.

CHAPTER FOUR

"P" is for Purpose

It seems painfully obvious that one would have to know a meeting's purpose before planning – let alone attending – it, right? Then how do you explain all those times you've found yourself 45 minutes into a gathering, glazing over at the sight of yet another slide presentation and wondering, *"Why am I here?"*

While we can't necessarily help you with the higher existential ramifications of that question, we can help you understand the importance of clearly defining the purpose of a meeting. Before you think too much about the purpose of your meeting, let's take a look at the purpose of meetings, in general.

We have meetings because face time is valuable and because meetings are intended to serve a very valid, meaningful purpose within the structure of our business world. Despite evidence to the contrary, the primary purpose of meetings is not to catch up on the social lives of other departments or admire the CEO's new tie – although the latter couldn't hurt, really.

The primary purpose of meetings, as a whole, is to interact with one another as a group with an eye toward accomplishing a defined task.

Meetings are useful and powerful tools when used as directed. Sometimes decision-making, administration functions, and communications depend on "live" human interaction requiring group discussion, contact, or resolution.

If At First You Don't Want To Meet... Don't

The first question you should ask when considering holding a meeting is whether or not the meeting is even necessary. Yes. You read that right. It is actually possible – perhaps even probable – that a meeting isn't the best way to accomplish the task.

Meetings should be held when they serve a specific function, not out of habit. If meetings are your primary method of communicating or administering, then it's time to re-examine your line of thinking. You probably don't need to call a meeting to announce that you've switched the office coffee to decaf. In fact, upon further examination, you probably want to avoid delivering that blow face-to-face with staffers, if only for matters of personal safety.

4 - "P" is for Purpose

You may want to be "hands on" and "human" to your colleagues, but too much face time can mean a waste of time for those attending unnecessary meetings. The resulting resentment from those whose days are crammed as it is doesn't bode well for any future meetings you call.

Instead, when appropriate, consider any of these alternatives to meetings. All are perfectly acceptable for conveying information and even, in some instances, soliciting ideas and opinions from smaller groups:

- Email
- Company Intranet/Bulletin Boards
- Memos
- Reports
- Telephone

Again, remember the point is to select the method that is the most efficient and convenient for all parties involved. Walk that fine line of being respectful of everyone's schedule but also understanding that people also need to be seen and heard at times.

Determining The Type Of Meeting

As much as you'd like to avoid squeezing another meeting into your schedule, you've come to the conclusion that the next phase of your big project simply can't be achieved without a meeting. Now you have to figure out what type of meeting you'll have. (No, "boring" is not an acceptable answer, no matter how accurate it may be.)

Most meetings fall into one or more of the following categories. Defining the type of meeting you'll have or attend helps determine your expectations, as well as keeping you focused on the tasks at hand.

Will the group be involved in

- Building the Team
- Planning a Project
- Solving a Problem
- Making a Decision
- Sharing Information
- Reviewing a Project
- Managing a Crisis
- Generating Ideas
- Celebrating an Accomplishment

Establishing the Purpose

If your usual meeting goal is to try to keep your eyelids in a propped and upright position, it's definitely an admirable one. However, let me assure you that once you define a very clear purpose, staying awake won't be a struggle.

One of the reasons meetings seem to go on and on and on without any clear goal is because no one sets any. Who knew? Once you determine what type of meeting to have, craft a purpose statement for your meeting. Be as specific as possible.

Compare the following examples of vague purpose statements and their more focused counterparts to give you an idea of what a difference it makes in the flow of a meeting:

Example 1

Meeting Type: Project Planning

Vague Purpose: Moving forward with the Jones Company

Specific Purpose: Determine the first three steps in securing a marketing partnership with the Jones Company; assign three people to head up further research to determine costs, logistics, and feasibility.

Example 2

Meeting Type: Decision-Making

Vague Purpose: Decide how to handle shipping orders for Dusty Flakes

Specific Purpose: Evaluate alternatives for handling shipping orders of Dusty Flakes, select the best option, and assign action steps so that we can streamline the process.

Once you've crafted the purpose statement, you'll have the beginnings of a roadmap that will keep your meeting moving in the right direction. With the purpose clearly in mind, you'll be able to design a *good* agenda.

So, let's move on to the next section, the "O" in our P.O.I.N.T. system, to find out how to do just that.

CHAPTER FIVE

"O" is for Organization

I f you've ever uttered the phrase, "Oh, well, I guess we'll just figure that out when we get to the meeting," you'd better have a seat. Believe it or not, you have now set the stage for a potential disaster. As we learned in the previous section, you have to know specifically why you're going to the meeting before you get within spitting distance of the boardroom. That means planning, and that also means – organization.

Organization is essential for all concerned. It's just good old-fashioned logic that the more organized the meeting, the better it flows and the more productive the time. By using a variety of structured activities and tools we can get the most out of our meetings and our people.

We tend to seriously underestimate the amount of time and planning that facilitators, presenters, and participants require in order to be fully prepared at meetings. Here, we'll walk you through some of the most important elements of organization when it comes to planning and attending meetings.

The Time Is Now

There is quite a bit of so-called conventional wisdom when it comes to the best day of the week and time of day to meet. Avoid Monday mornings, since no one has hit their stride yet, but don't wait until Friday, when they're already thinking about the weekend. Don't do it first thing in the morning or at the end of the day. Not before lunch, but not right after lunch, either.

If we followed these "rules," we'd have about five minutes on Wednesday, around mid-morning, when we could all meet. It's far more likely that meeting times pick us and not the other way around. We meet when we're free, or at least when the majority of participants are free.

In other words, there's no "rule" about what time is best to meet but you know your colleague's work habits – peaks and valleys – as well as anyone. Schedule accordingly. And unless it's completely unavoidable, schedule meetings within normal business hours. There's no better way to guarantee an unreceptive and unresponsive group of attendees than to drag them into corporate workspace on a Saturday afternoon.

Length Matters: Keeping It Short

One of the most common complaints we hear is that meetings run on too long. On the other side of that argument, you have the meeting planners waving agendas wildly, certain that disaster will ensue if all is not crammed into one three-hour meeting marathon.

Sure, it may be more convenient on paper to gather everyone together once instead of three times throughout the month (or week), but efficiency gets tossed completely out the window when a meeting drags on. What's the point in keeping your best minds captive if they flatline after 45 minutes?

We tend to think of our days as being divided into 30- and 60-minute increments: meetings, lunches, errands. All falling on the hour or half hour, lasting for an hour or half hour. No one says you have to hold a 30-minute meeting if you can get it all done in 20. Who wouldn't appreciate wrapping it up as quickly as possible?

Shoot for about 45-60 minutes maximum for your meeting. If it's entirely impossible to avoid a longer meeting, give your attendees short breaks at 60-minute intervals. What's the point in stretching it out if the audience is waning and their energy is sapped? They need to be refreshed and you'll get far more done if you have everyone's attention.

(Another good way to trim time off meetings is to revisit the previous chapter on Purpose. See if there isn't information that could be presented in another form – report, memo, email – before the meeting, rather than during.)

Besides, if your meeting has a P.O.I.N.T., you shouldn't need to run over time anyway.

Your New Best Friend: The Agenda

This is your ultimate organizing tool – and the thing entirely too many meetings lack. It's the agenda – and if you learn how to pull a good one together, your meetings will practically run themselves. (Practically.)

Note that the operative word in the sentence above is "good." After all, there are agendas…and there are *good* agendas. The latter is one crucial element in ensuring your meetings are productive, efficient, and focused.

A good agenda outlines clearly the who, what, where, and when (so to speak) of your meeting and if properly planned and diligently followed, it will dazzle your meeting participants with its simple effectiveness.

Remember that the agenda isn't just for your own benefit – although feel free to frame your favorites and hang them in your cubicle. It is a powerful organizational tool that lets everyone know what the meeting is about and what's expected of them. It can also be a handy list at the end of the meeting for reviewing and making sure you covered everything.

The Elements Of Your Agenda

Pulling together a good agenda is not the corporate equivalent of baking a soufflé. Rather, it's a simple, handy, tried-and-true recipe that works out perfectly each time, as long as you stick to it.

5 - "O" is for Organization

First, you'll need a list of topics to be covered at the meeting – but you've already started thinking about that during the Purpose stage.

Now, the ingredients you'll need on hand are:

1. Time allocated for each topic
2. Topic leader
3. Objective of the topic
4. Method to be used to achieve objective

So here's the scenario: it's fallen on you to pull together the agenda for a meeting to determine a new meeting venue. Referring to the elements listed above, items 1 and 2 are pretty straightforward – you should know precisely who will be addressing the issue or leading the discussion of that particular topic as well as how much time they have to do so.

The objective of the topic may have been determined when you reviewed the Purpose of your meeting. If not, now's the time to get specific about your expectations. For this meeting, you might be seeking any of the following outcomes: "a commitment by three volunteers to research the alternatives," "a list of alternatives," or "a decision regarding a new venue."

Again, be clear, specific and realistic about your goals. Organize the topics in a logical manner and plan to cover only what is realistic for the timeframe allotted.

The last item refers to the type of participation (or method) required from the group to achieve your desired objective. The method in this case could be a *report* from a committee member, a *discussion* to generate alternatives or a *decision* to finalize the discussion. Here are a couple of options for your agenda item:

Topic	Time	Topic Leader	Objective	Participation
Scenario 1				
New Meeting Venue	15 min.	Ida	List of Alternatives. Commitment from one volunteer to research these alternatives.	Brainstorming
Scenario 2				
New Meeting Venue	10 min.	Sandy	Report from volunteer. Decision by group.	Discussion Decision-making

Getting The Word Out

It is highly recommended that you get your agenda out to all expected participants well in advance of the meeting, usually a week and usually by email. (Plan to have hard copies at the meetings, too. Not everyone will remember to bring his or her email copy.)

5 - "O" is for Organization

Distributing the agenda ahead of time gives participants an opportunity

- to review the topics and any relevant background information,
- to understand precisely what is expected of them (opinions, creative problem-solving, brainstorming, etc.),
- to prepare, and
- to plan.

These last two points warrant special emphasis: prepare and plan. If you need creative and innovative brainstorming and problem-resolution, you have to encourage the free flow of ideas. When was the last time you were inspired by a meeting room (many with no windows and poor ventilation) or an office cubicle? Sitting around a board room table just doesn't do it for *me*.

By sending out the agenda ahead of time, you give your participants "thinking time". Creative ideas often materialize when we least expect them – and when we're engaged in an unrelated activity, such as driving to work, listening to a sermon, jogging around the neighborhood, taking a shower, cutting the lawn, and so on. So send those agendas out well ahead of time. The benefits? More participation, richer discussions, more creative solutions.

The Ground Rules

It can take years to master the written – and unwritten – "rules of the game" in business, but it doesn't take long to understand why the rules exist. Without them, it's chaos. No protocol. No clear lines for discussion and dissent. Meetings should be no different.

A key organizational element of successful meetings is the establishment of solid ground rules. Of course, establishing them is only meaningful if these guidelines are understood, respected, and followed by all members of a meeting – regardless of management level or stature.

If your group usually groans as soon as it hears the word "rules," then consider renaming them to "working agreements". This label may more accurately reflect your intent – to create an environment in which the participants work well together. That means sharing an understanding of the behavior expected of all group members.

Sometimes establishing these working agreements or ground rules can be more freeing than restricting. With the right structure and a clear understanding of boundaries, meeting participants will be less anxious about expectations, more open with their contributions, and more relaxed.

In order to ensure buy-in and cooperation, have your group establish its own set of rules or agreements. Here are some that other groups have used.

The meeting starts on time

Waiting around for latecomers or no-shows can make those who showed up on time feel put off. Plus, logic dictates that if you start late, you end late. Show everyone how important their time – and yours – is by starting on time. Stragglers will soon learn that you're serious about your timelines.

Turn off beepers and cell phones

This goes for *everyone*. You'll get far more done if you minimize distractions and interruptions. Once a participant makes a commitment to attend a meeting, it should take temporary priority over outside issues.

Limit socializing and discourage cross talk

It's nice to encourage a warm social environment, but that's not the purpose of your meeting. Besides, if you let some people get buddy-buddy, it just makes it apparent who's *not* included – and that's not conducive to a productive atmosphere. Similarly, cross talk is distracting and – have we mentioned this before? – makes the meeting last looooooooonger.

Stick to the agenda and stay on topic

Cover everything on the agenda, but put items for future meetings into a "Parking Lot". Acknowledge all points as valid, but discussion should remain strictly focused on the topic at hand.

Meeting with Success

Participate in a constructive manner

Let people know that participation, where appropriate, is encouraged but set some boundaries if necessary. Everyone's input must be treated with equal respect – and, if possible, without judgment. Interrupting others and making negative comments (e.g. snide remarks) are behaviors you might want to outlaw outright.

Be concise and to the point

Again, this goes for everyone. Accept feedback or comments only where indicated as appropriate on the agenda.

Keeping Records

The meeting is about to begin and you see the facilitator looking around, dry-erase marker or legal pad in hand. You look the other way, but it doesn't work. He's seen you. He's coming your way. It's too late. You've been picked to take the meeting's minutes.

Where's your team spirit? After all, this is precisely the type of task you'd have been vying for in second grade. Maybe things are a little different now. Besides, taking minutes means you not only have to stay awake throughout the entire meeting but it means you have to pay attention. What kind of a deal is that?

Actually, in our book, it's a pretty good one. If you're asking yourself why we should be taking minutes at meetings and reading them at subsequent ones, it's time to take a step back and re-examine this vital organizational tool.

5 - "O" is for Organization

Minutes are part of the overall paper trail that helps to serve several purposes, most notably to keep meetings focused, gauge a meeting's effectiveness, track all major decisions, eradicate post-meeting confusion, and (yippee!) improve the efficiency of future gatherings.

Here is a sample template for recording all important aspects of the meeting.

Meeting Minutes				
Recorded by _____				
Date:	Time:	Place:	Attendees:	Absentees:
Scheduled by:		Purpose:		
Agenda Item	Action / Decision		Assigned To:	By When:
Items for Next Meeting's Agenda:	Notes:			

Meeting with Success

Minutes should be distributed as soon after the meeting as possible while the topics are still fresh in everyone's mind. Any corrections or clarifications can then be made quickly and efficiently.

CHAPTER SIX

"I" is for Involvement

You can have the most amazing agenda on earth and the most solid objectives – and it can all fall by the wayside in action if you don't have a foolproof set of techniques and your finger on the pulse of your participants. (Not literally, of course.)

People – and the techniques you use to draw them in – can make or break the meeting. Hence, the third fundamental P.O.I.N.T. element of a successful meeting lies in Involvement – the "who" and "how" of meeting participants.

Mr. Jones Requests The Honor Of Your Presence...

The first people-related issue facing you is who to invite to your meeting. Remember, this isn't the social event of the season so you needn't worry about hurt feelings. (Chances are, no matter how fabulous your presentations are rumored to be, most people would rather skip any meeting.)

A common complaint among meeting participants is that they don't know why they're at the meeting. Remember the purpose of your meeting and review your objectives. Invite only those participants absolutely necessary for you to achieve your goals.

If the *outcome* of the meeting affects a large number of people, you can inform them of the results after the meeting by memo, email or report. You can even schedule a very brief informational follow-up meeting if you think face time is merited. But there's no need to zap the productivity of 40 staffers for an hour. We all attend too many meetings as it is. Plan to invite only those who will be directly involved with your objective.

Who Are The People In Your Neighborhood?

Understanding roles, personalities, and how those affect the productivity of meetings has a huge impact on a meeting's overall effectiveness. No matter where you work, no matter your line of business, we all attend meetings along with a cast of regular characters. Thank goodness some people are so predictable! Knowing who's who is essential to being fully prepared. Here are some of the usual suspects and how to best handle them. See if you recognize your colleagues – or yourself – in the following descriptions.

The Rambler

Need we say more? Always eager to contribute, it doesn't matter how much preparation he has done or keen insight he brings to the topic at hand – it's all diluted by the fact that he doesn't know when to quit. He's particularly unpopular in meetings, where he single-handedly doubles the meeting time. The Rambler is best dealt with politely and firmly, by leveraging the Ground Rules. "That's an excellent point, Albert, but we're at the three-minute mark so I'll have to move things along."

The Interrupter

No one gets a sentence out without The Interrupter doing her job. As often or not, she's injecting objections or discounting opinions. In fact, the mere fact that she interrupts discredits those who are speaking. She's clearly an annoyance and a source of tension. Again, Ground Rules should be set up to ban all interruptions and others should lead by example.

The Pusher

What's this character pushing? His opinion. On everyone. More timid participants simply clam up when he's around, knowing he'll just try to railroad them. They're too intimidated to stand up to him. He's the reason meeting rules matter, but his behavior may require addressing outside the meeting, too.

The Skeptic

Not as forceful as The Pusher, The Skeptic nonetheless has a huge effect on the attitude of meeting participants. No idea gets past The Skeptic without her shaking her head, burrowing her eyebrows, or expressing why this won't work. She's genuinely concerned about the project at hand, but her thought pattern runs to the negative. Encourage her to think from a different perspective.

The Side Talker

For The Side Talker, there's always something more interesting to gab about than the matter at hand. He delivers a constant barrage of side comments, often to reluctant recipients. He's not necessarily saying anything harmful, but his actions are disrespectful and distracting. A useful technique to use in this situation is body language – move slowly into his space. He'll begin to feel uncomfortable as he senses your close proximity. You might also try pausing in mid-sentence or if someone else is doing the talking ask them to pause for a moment. When the side talker realizes he's the only one talking, he'll stop.

The Coma People

We can all fall into this category if a meeting is bad enough. Coma People glaze over, phase out, doodle, sketch, bring other work to the meeting – whatever they're doing, it's not focused on the topic at hand. Proper meeting planning can virtually eliminate the problem, as can using the proper techniques to help keep everyone involved.

Conflict & Resolution

They are the bane of every meeting – the arguments, the sniping, people jumping across the table to throttle others. Okay, so sometimes it's the most entertaining part but it's certainly not productive when heated arguments throw the meeting off track and prevent progress.

It's one of the inherent problems when involving multiple personalities with multiple agendas in your meeting but arguments can be avoided or, at the very least, minimized by creating and adhering to a meeting environment that doesn't allow them to emerge in the first place.

Just remember, there is a key difference between arguing and disagreeing. The former is disruptive, while the latter is actually an essential part of generating good business ideas and keeping everyone creative. Keep it respectful and remember the Ground Rules. Lay a foundation that supports constructive exchange of ideas.

Encouraging Involvement

So just how do you build this foundation of constructive involvement? The key to making it more than a theory lies in adopting and using the right techniques to get what you want out of your meeting participants.

You'll use these tried and true techniques (or structured activities) to generate ideas, analyze situations, solve problems, and make decisions. They also help keep personalities in check, build on other's ideas, improve overall listening skills, and increase participation levels. When attendees are involved they tend to feel a greater sense of ownership and partnership in the matters at hand.

Something as seemingly minor as using first names, letting your participants know they matter and their opinions are valued is all the encouragement reluctant participants need to chime in and be a part of the show. Ask specific questions of your participants to encourage interaction. Focus on what matters to your participants. They're unlikely to get involved if the topic doesn't affect them directly.

Creativity Tools For Idea Generation

An ongoing element of most successful businesses is the creative generation of new ideas, whether it's to determine which potential clients to pursue or what color to paint the boardroom.

One of the most common methods is brainstorming, where participants are encouraged to contribute ideas in a rapid-fire, no-holds-barred exchange. Often, however, brainstorming digresses into a never-ending exercise that results in more confusion than inspiration. There are few things as discouraging as gearing up for The Big Creative Ideas and winding up with a room full of blank stares. If you want to generate creativity, you have to foster the right environment.

Before we discuss specific creative techniques, here are some tips for having the most creative and productive brainstorming and idea generating meetings.

Change of place, not pace

Consider the environment in which the meeting is taking place. Your company may have shelled out thousands for a state-of-the-art boardroom, but that doesn't necessarily make it the best place. If possible, consider a change of venue – meet outside, at a pizza parlor or the golf course. Sometimes, if you want people to think outside the box, you have to take them outside the box.

The key is picking locations that provide more inspiration than distraction and following your ground rules no matter where you are.

Keep it interesting

Even if you're stuck in the boardroom, you can up creativity and fuel minds by using visuals and graphics to stimulate ideas. Use presentation tools, cartoons and appropriate humor to help people think differently. For example, if you're trying to generate tag lines for a new product, bring along pictures of the product from different angles, photos of typical customers, the products in use, competitive products – anything that might inspire that one winning idea.

Ground rules, ground rules, ground rules

The idea is to generate as many ideas as possible – without judgment – in a given period of time. Make sure no one is allowed to assign values to the ideas of others – evaluation occurs later, often in a separate session. Focus on the ideas, not the people who generate them.

Toys

Children are far more creative in their thinking, generally speaking, than grown ups, thanks to their lack of inhibitions when it comes to playing. That's the spirit you can recapture with the right toys and props. Now, we're not advocating a food fight at the sales meeting, but just the visual and tactile stimulation of having toys around – Koosh balls, stress balls, Slinkies, Silly Putty, pipe cleaners – can be inspiration. The key is to have colorful toys that keep the hands occupied – and the mind free to tackle the problem at hand.

Keep good records

We're as big on record keeping as we are on ground rules. Keep track of all ideas that are generated in the session. Good ideas aren't always evident at first and the best ideas can have holes in them that aren't immediately apparent. You can't afford to throw away any potential gold mines.

Now Think Creatively

Okay, now you have some general guidelines to follow. Bear those in mind as you explore some of the following specific group process techniques for getting creative.

Brainstorming

It's one of the most common forms of idea generation. The point of brainstorming is to get people to come up with as many ideas as possible in a certain amount of time, without being restricted or inhibited. There are a few guidelines for getting the most out of your brainstorming sessions:

1. Make sure everyone knows what it is they're trying to brainstorm – what the goal is, what the problem is.
2. Ideas should be generated without judgment. That means no negative comments, no value assigned to notions. Each should be given equal weight.
3. This is about coming up with ideas, not discussing them. Unless something needs clarification, keep going.
4. Encourage people to build on the ideas generated by others.
5. Record all your ideas – you never know where the good ones come from.

Don't stop just because you've reached a good idea. Keep going. You might get something better!

Making it Even More Effective

There are many variations on the brainstorming method. Here are some suggestions for getting more from the group during a brainstorming session.

- **Divide the participants up** into groups of 2, 3, or 4 and have them brainstorm amongst themselves. You'll get many more ideas within the same timeframe and you'll give the quieter members an opportunity to express themselves. (This is also a good technique for evening out the playing field, or in other words, reducing the unwanted impact of some of the personalities we looked at earlier.)

- Have the participants record each idea on an **index card,** large sticky note, or slip of paper. Then post them on a board or wall for all to see. This makes for easier discussion, categorizing, and prioritization.

- Or, instead of posting the ideas, have everyone **deposit** their written **suggestions into a container** (hat, bowl, box). Then as each item is drawn out of the container, the group discusses the pros and cons of the suggestion. This technique focuses attention away from the author of the idea and onto the idea itself. This technique works best in situations with a relatively small number of people and ideas.

- A further variation on this technique has the individuals **passing their written suggestions around the group** so others can add comments. This technique is based on the notion that the best ideas come from building on the ideas of one another.

- Stimulate thought by asking people to **visualize** the outcomes. What would it look like in the ideal state? How would it function?

- Finally, a technique for those of us who already think backwards – Reversal!

6 - "I" is for Involvement

› **Ask the opposite** - Here's the key to the technique: instead of asking the questions you want to ask, you ask the opposite. Got it? Here's an example: Instead of asking how you could increase revenue, ask yourselves how you could *decrease* revenue. Give concrete, specific answers, such as: "Spend more money on meeting snacks" or "Use the most expensive travel agent."

› **Examine the answers** - Next, you'll use these "answers" to take a look at your current spending and make sure you're not doing those things. *Are* you spending more on meeting snacks? *Is* your travel agent too expensive? The Reversal process not only gives you a different perspective but also often highlights a course of action that perhaps should have seemed obvious but has been overlooked.

› **Implement -** Once you've identified the areas for improvement or action, well, you know the drill – now you're primed to develop an action plan, then implement, implement, implement.

Decision-Making & Problem-Solving Techniques

If your eyes are rolling back in your head as you start reading this paragraph, you're like most of us who have sat through decision-making and problem-solving meetings where nothing is accomplished but wasting time.

The right techniques can make sure the right decisions are made, effectively and efficiently. Before you begin, define clearly for everyone who is making the decision and how it will be made. For example:

- Is the purpose of the group to foster discussion so that the chairman can make a decision based upon the arguments?

- Will you be presenting information to a group who will make the decision?

- Will the decision be made by group consensus or majority vote?

Once you have made that determination, following these decisionreaching steps can smooth the process and make sure everyone stays focused and on track:

1. Clearly **define the question** at hand. People often think they know what they're working toward when they're actually off base. Don't be afraid to come back to defining the issue at hand as many times as necessary to ensure the decision-making process goes smoothly?

2. Ask people to **contribute alternative options** and follow meeting ground rules for respectful and timely discussion of all ideas.

3. Work as a group to **evaluate these ideas**. The key here is to once again separate the ideas from the people who generate them. Making a decision is a common goal and arguments should be based on facts, not opinion.

4. Once each option has been evaluated, it's **time for a decision**. If it's a group decision, select a voting method that everyone's most comfortable with – usually a show of hands will do, but sensitive issues may require a "silent" vote to protect the reputations and comfort levels of voters.

5. Determine **how this decision will be implemented**. It's not enough to reach a decision. You have to know how you're going to make it happen and put it into play.

6. Determine how **future evaluations** of this decision will occur. It's essential that you have a method for revisiting your decision and gauging its effectiveness.

Six Thinking Hats

We commonly refer to wearing different "hats" as a figurative term for the different roles we play. These "hats" we speak of represent different perspectives. The Six Thinking Hats technique (developed by Edward de Bono) borrows from that idea.

Meeting with Success

The technique provides six clearly defined different ways of looking at a problem or issue to help us break out of our normal, sometimes rather limited thinking patterns.

Ask your participants to intentionally think from a different perspective:

- with facts and data only
- straight from the gut (emotionally)
- from the negative point of view (the Skeptic will love this)
- from a positive perspective (What's good about this idea?)
- from an uninhibited creative perspective
- about the thinking that is taking place

Pareto Chart

It only sounds like something your doctor examines but this technique is actually for helping you determine the changes that need to be made with your product or process. It all revolves around the Pareto Principle – that 20% of the work can generate 80% of the advantage of doing the entire job. (The method was named after Vilifredo Pareto, the Italian economist who originally contended that 80% of the world's wealth was held by 20% of its people.) In other words, you're looking to make fewer changes with bigger benefits.

List the problems or options you're looking at and discuss possible changes that you could make. Where

6 - "I" is for Involvement

appropriate, group together similar changes in order to simplify the process. Based on your goal, score each of the possible changes you could make in terms of its overall importance.

Now, step back and take a look at the changes or options, tackling those with the highest score first. By dealing with the most important changes, you can reassess the options with lowest scores and determine whether or not they're even worth addressing. In other words, solve the big problems and the little problems no longer even seem to matter.

For example, a restaurant manager empties out the restaurant's suggestion box and finds the following: four cards saying his employees were rude, one card saying the food was cold, one saying the food was too expensive and two cards saying the restrooms are dirty. The manager's overall goal is to increase customer satisfaction.

The manager lays the cards out in front of him, grouping together the complaints. He assigns them a score – or worth – based on the number of complaints he has received for each category:

- Customer service complaints – 4
- Restrooms – 2
- Food quality – 1
- Food pricing – 1

Obviously, the number one issue to be dealt with – the biggest problem at hand – is the attitude of his workers. Next is the

Meeting with Success

cleanliness of the restrooms, followed by the food quality concern.

Now that he has prioritized his problems, he can come up with solutions, first for the customer service problems (perhaps more training, new incentives, etc.).

Next, he can plan a check system to make sure the restrooms are kept up properly. Once those two larger issues are resolved, the single food quality complaint becomes more of a statistical anomaly than anything else. He has processed change in the areas that will have the biggest impact.

Alternative Scenarios

The Alternative Scenarios method involves looking at a number of different possible scenarios in order to get a broader understanding of the situation at hand and a fuller perspective on the issues.

In addition, imagining Alternative Scenarios helps you prepare for the future, as you can determine which factors need to be closely monitored and you'll develop potential plans for all kinds of outcomes. Thinking this way really forces people to get more creative and be more broad-minded than their current "reality" may.

Here's how to use it:

1. Oh, you know this one – specifically identify the decision you're trying to make or the problem that needs to be solved.

6 - "I" is for Involvement

2. Identify the "environmental forces" – those beyond your company's control that affect the issue at hand – consumer trends, economy, competition. Try to think beyond the obvious. The more in-depth you are, the more effective the Alternative Scenarios technique will be.

3. Take each of the environmental forces you've identified and try to come up with three or four possible scenarios that involve each force. For example, come up with four different ways changes in consumer trends could affect your business – both positive and negative. For example, consumer trends could make the demand for your service higher or it could dwindle considerably.

4. Now that you have these Alternative Scenarios use them to come up with "story lines" that outline how you can respond to each individual scenario. How would you handle a sudden increase in demand for your service? What would you do if your customer base threatened to drop off by 35%?

5. Step back from the different Alternative Scenarios you've come up with and examine them. Look for patterns, issues that connect across several different forces. Find common areas of concern or potential for growth to help you determine the best solution or option and how to implement it.

Analysis – Assessing the Idea Generating Efforts

If you've just completed an idea generating/brainstorming session, you're probably looking at a wall full of ideas. The task now is to determine how to plow through all of this effectively.

Consider having a separate meeting for assessing the brainstorming session or the ideas generated. It helps everyone separate the ideas from people who came up with them and allows analysis without blame.

Try these tips:

- Have everyone select a number – five or so – of ideas they like best.

- Ask them to further clarify their preferences by prioritizing them in order of which they like most.

- Group these ideas together to narrow down the focus.

- Clarify the factors that are most important in evaluating each idea (For example, cost, timeframe, feasibility)

- Once you've clearly established these criteria, assess each idea and be realistic. The most popular idea, after all, may not be workable.

- Determine the best idea or ideas for implementation.

6 - "I" is for Involvement

- If needed, resort back to some of the decision-making techniques to "decide" on how much value things have. Don't be afraid to assign scores based on what's most important to you and your goals and let the numbers dictate the outcome.

Meeting with Success

CHAPTER SEVEN

"N" is for Navigation

Anyone who wants to get anywhere needs to know where they're going, how to get there and how to stay focused. That's where the "N" in P.O.I.N.T. comes in – Navigation – focus and direction, usually provided by a navigator – or in business speak, a facilitator.

You have two options. You may wish to consider bringing in a professional meeting facilitator – an impartial third party who will orchestrate the show – someone who is trained in facilitation techniques and who will help you get over the bumpy spots. The other alternative is to draw from within the organization, where there are often plenty of natural born meeting facilitators. They as well can be trained in the skills necessary to run great meetings.

The facilitator's job is to ensure the task is accomplished while at the same time creating a good working

Meeting with Success

relationship among the participants. She provides insights and feedback to the group that affect both of these aspects of the meeting.

Unfortunately, we often notice good navigation and strong leadership when it's absent rather than when it's present. When we're under the influence of a strong navigator, the meeting tends to flow so smoothly we don't notice the facilitation itself. That's how it should be and even though it helps to have specific individuals handle the task, everyone at a meeting should be prepared to do his or her own part to keep things rolling along.

Here is a checklist of "musts" in order for the meeting to run successfully. After all, your killer agenda and techniques mean nothing if you don't have an individual or individuals committed to making sure everything is...you guessed it, implemented. An effective facilitator should:

- Be prepared for the meeting at hand. There should be no surprises for the facilitator at the meeting. If the facilitator isn't responsible for pulling together the agenda, she needs to make sure she understands everything on it. Not at the meeting – beforehand.

- Have a thorough and workable knowledge of creative, problem solving and decision-making techniques.

- Provide and distribute information to all participants before and after the meeting. This includes:

7 - "N" is for Navigation

> Objectives of meeting
> Agenda
> Location
> Date
> Time
> Any and all pertinent background information

The facilitator should also send out a reminder email a day before the meeting and solicit feedback after the meeting.

- Know who is attending the meeting ahead of time and, if key players are unavailable, determine whether or not to reschedule the meeting.

- Make sure the meeting starts – and ends – on time. Start out by closing the meeting doors at the stated beginning time and announcing that you understand everyone's schedule is important so you'll appreciate everyone's cooperation in keeping to the schedule.

- Clearly state the reason for the meeting. Greet everyone with, "Welcome. The purpose of today's meeting is…" This will avoid any confusion right from the start.

- Review the ground rules before each meeting, letting everyone know how decisions will be made and what the expectations are of the participants.

- Understand the people. This includes knowing who all the participants are as well as, if possible, their relationship with each other. Make sure everyone knows each other, providing introductions as necessary.

- Assign tasks or roles to participants and ensure they're accomplished. (See details in next chapter.)

- Make sure the meeting stays focused on the task, objectives, and goals at hand. That doesn't mean ignoring ideas or comments of participants that may not be entirely relevant at the moment. It's important that people feel valued. Record their ideas on a "Parking Lot" for addition later in the meeting or at a separate meeting entirely.

- Deal effectively with disruptions and any personality issues using the techniques outlined in the section on Involvement.

- Maintain a tone of honesty and openness, listening to others and encouraging an environment in which ideas can be exchanged freely. Using humor can help set a great mood for even greater decisions.

- Recognize when he or she is not the right person to facilitate, surrendering such duties to a more appropriate party, always keeping the company's best interest in mind.

7 - "N" is for Navigation

- End each meeting with a recap of how things went, summarizing all decisions, making sure all tasks are assigned, confirming assignments, due dates, time lines and any other action items.

- Make time at the end of each meeting to evaluate the meeting's effectiveness. Use a questionnaire to help pinpoint the areas for improvement and to encourage honest and open feedback.

Meeting with Success

CHAPTER EIGHT

"T" is for Tasks

Tasks. Assignments. Roles. No matter what you call them, they're the final element in making sure your meeting has a P.O.I.N.T. Of course, being last doesn't mean it's least important. In fact, proper understanding of the tasks to be accomplished before, during, and after the meeting is essential to your gathering's success.

The following are some of the most common meeting roles and the responsibilities – or tasks – that each faces.

Facilitator

If you skipped the last chapter, you're just going to have to go back and start over. (Isn't that always the case?) The facilitator has plenty of tasks at hand, each as important as the next. Among them is, usually, the task of taking responsibility for making sure everyone else understands – and completes – *their*

Meeting with Success

tasks. So, if you find yourself being assigned an active role in a meeting, instead of complaining about it, just be grateful you're not the facilitator.

Here are a few of the facilitator's tasks.

Before	During	After
Prepare agenda. Notify participant. Check with topic leaders.	Obtain approval of the agenda. Direct the flow of the meeting. Encourage active listening and participation. Keep people on track (remember the ground rules and various personalities). Summarize discussions and decisions. Delegate tasks. Set date and agenda for next meeting.	Follow-up with absent participants. Complete personal action items.

8 - "T" is for Tasks

Participants

Contrary to popular belief, it's not enough just to show up at a meeting. Everyone at a meeting is equally responsible for ensuring that all goes well. Consider asking yourself, "What am I doing to help or hinder this group from achieving its objective?"

Here is a list of participant responsibilities:

Before	During	After
Complete assigned action items.	Arrive on time.	Support group decisions publicly.
Prepare materials and reports for the meeting.	Adhere to the ground rules.	Complete personal action items or inform facilitator if unable to do so.
Read agenda and understand the purpose of the meeting.	Bring all relevant materials to the meeting.	Provide progress reports to the facilitator as necessary.
Be prepared to discuss all agenda items.	Participate actively and constructively and encourage others to do the same.	
Inform facilitator or minute taker if you are unable to attend the meeting.	Use good listening skills.	
	Avoid disruptive behaviours (playing the part of the Skeptic, Side Talker, etc.)	

Meeting with Success

Before	During	After
	Ask for clarification when needed. Help monitor the agenda and keep the discussions on track. Note personal action items.	

Time Keeper

Talk about power! Time is one of the things we value most and the person in charge of keeping it has the controls. Before you get any devious ideas about ruling the world, the role of the timekeeper is to make sure that the meeting, well, keeps time.

His observations about time allotted versus time needed can be essential in planning an agenda and increasing the productivity of future meetings.

During
Assist the facilitator in ensuring the meeting starts and ends on time.
Keep track of time allocated for each agenda item.
Ensure each topic receives the fair amount of time it deserves – suggest adjustments as necessary.
Give the facilitator sufficient notice before time is up.

Minute Taker

This is a task that requires a great deal of attention, not to mention neutrality. The ideal candidate will be on his or her proverbial toes during the meeting keeping track of everything that goes on. (Refer to the section under Organization entitled "Keeping Records" for a useful template.)

During	After
Obtain approval for the minutes from the last meeting. Take attendance. Record action items, timelines, and people responsible. Record decisions, problems resolved, and new business to be addressed. Ask for clarification as necessary.	Prepare minutes for distribution. Distribute the minutes to all attending and absent members of the group within 24 hours of the meeting.

Meeting with Success

CHAPTER NINE

Into Action

Business wisdom indicates that theories and solutions mean nothing if they aren't put into action. Not surprisingly, that holds true for just about everything you've read in the previous pages. The truth is, you really can make drastic changes in your meetings – in fact, your mind's probably already brimming with ideas.

The P.O.I.N.T. system makes it easy to remember and employ the elements of a good meeting. To recap (as all good facilitators do):

- **P** urpose
- **O** rganization
- **I** nvolvement
- **N** avigation
- **T** asks

Meeting with Success

Learn it. Share it. Live it. Friends, you have the tools to run focused productive meetings. Now it's time to put them into action – and start thinking about what you'll do with all the extra time on your hands.

Good luck!

Bibliography

Bens, Ingrid (2000). *Facilitating With Ease!* San Francisco: Jossey-Bass Publishers.

Brassard, Michael & Ritter, Diane (1994). *The Memory Jogger II.* Methuen, MA: GOAL/QPC.

De Bono, Edward (1985). *Six Thinking Hats.* Boston: Little, Brown and Company.

Field, Mary Blitzer (2000). *Meeting Repair Kit.* King of Prussia, Pennsylvania: HRDQ.

Higgins, James M. (1994). *101 Creative Problem Solving Techniques.* Winter Park, Florida: The New Management Publishing Company.

Mosvick, R., & Nelson, R. (1996). *We've Got to Start Meeting Like This!* Indianapolis, Indiana: Park Avenue.

Pyle, Laura (1991). *Meeting Effectiveness Questionnaire*. Ann Arbor, Michigan: Aviat a division of Orion International Ltd.

Schwarz, Roger M. (1994). *The Skilled Facilitator*. San Francisco: Jossey-Bass Publishers.

Stanfield, R. Brian (2000) (Ed.). *The Art of Focused Conversation*. Toronto: The Canadian Institute for Cultural Affairs.

Thompson, Charles "Chic" (1992). *What a Great Idea!* New York: HarperCollins Publishers.

About the Author

Ida Shessel, B.Sc., M.Ed., is the president of Let Us Facilitate. She has more than 20 years of experience as a facilitator in the business and academic sectors.

Ida facilitates meetings and training programs that are results-driven, focused, and productive. More than 6,000 participants have benefited from the techniques that she uses in her meetings and workshops.

Meeting with Success

Contact Ida Shessel about her training programs in effective meeting skills; other publications and audio programs on running focused, productive meetings; and facilitation, speaking, and consulting services.

Telephone: +1 (905) 882-5278

Email: ida@letusfacilitate.com

Web: http://www.letusfacilitate.com
             http://www.absolutelygreatmeetings.com

Other Books by Ida Shessel

74 Tips for Absolutely Great Teleconference Meetings.

77 Tips for Absolutely Great Meetings.

79 Tips for Absolutely Great Teleclasses.

Meeting with Success Workbook.

For more information on these titles, visit
www.letusfacilitate.com

Meeting with Success

Become a conference call superstar!

With the proliferation of teleconference meetings in today's distributed team environment, many organizations now conduct most of their meetings over the telephone. There are challenges associated with trying to ensure that these meetings are productive and successful.

74 Tips for Absolutely Great Teleconference Meetings contains tips for both the teleconference leader and the participant — tips on how to prepare for the teleconference, start the teleconference meeting and set the tone, lead the teleconference, keep participants away from their e-mail during the call, use voice and language effectively, and draw the teleconference to a close. The book also includes a helpful checklist you can use to assess what you need to do to make your teleconference meetings more effective.

Mastering the art of holding a good meeting is one sure-fire way to get recognized as a leader by your peers and your management. Being able to hold an *absolutely great* teleconference meeting positions you as a leader who can also leverage modern technologies to improve efficiency. Develop this career-building skill by ordering this book today!

Available in electronic formats from most ebook online retailers or directly from the publisher at **www.mmpubs.com**.

Make people *yearn* to attend your meetings!

Turn dull meetings into dynamic group experiences! Chances are that you spend a lot of time at meetings - some are focused and productive, while others are not. This ebook, written by a professional facilitator, contains 77 tips for both meeting leaders and participants. Implementing one or more of these tips can produce dramatic results at your meetings.

Learn how to strengthen your leadership abilities, plan effectively, use structure to get more from your meetings, manage group dynamics, empower yourself and others to become strong contributors to the meeting, and more. Inside this ebook there is even a helpful checklist that you can use to assess what you need to do to make your meetings more effective.

Our work life revolves around meetings - make yours the most effective they can be.

Available in electronic formats from most ebook online retailers or directly from the publisher at **www.mmpubs.com**.

Distance learning can be effective AND fun.

Are you struggling to find ways to keep the interest of your teleclass and webinar attendees? How do you make these distance learning sessions both informative and entertaining?

Using her years of expertise as a distance learning specialist, author Ida Shessel reveals the secrets to planning, hosting, and conducting telephone-based education for your staff and your customers.

Learn how to plan a teleclass to use the available technology most effectively, get the call started and quickly establish rapport with the attendees, create an effective learning environment (and minimize distractions), end the call effectively, and follow up to solidify the benefits from the call. Along the way, you will learn how to use your voice and language effectively; this is important because, without you being physically present in front of the class, your words and voice are all you have to convey meaning.

Read the book that is capturing the attention of trainers, professional speakers, and other business professionals.

Available in print and electronic formats from most online retailers or directly from the publisher at **www.mmpubs.com**.

Changing Jobs? Get Started on the Right Foot

Studies show that your working relationship with the boss is one of the top factors in job satisfaction. Whether you have a new job, or a new boss in your current job, you need to focus on building a solid working relationship with this very important person in your work life.

This ebook by human resources guru Peter R. Garber gives you tips on how to forge a positive relationship and get on the good side of your new boss. Start out on the right foot and read this book today!

ISBN: 1-897326-18-1   (Adobe Acrobat PDF)
ISBN: 1-897326-19-X   (Microsoft Reader LIT)
ISBN: 1-897326-20-3   (Palm Reader PDB)
ISBN: 1-897326-21-1   (Mobipocket Reader PRC)

Order from all major online ebook retailers, or direct from the publisher at **www.mmpubs.com**

Need More Help with the Politics at Work?

100 Ways To Get On The Wrong Side Of Your Boss (And Strategies to Prevent You from Getting There!) was written for anyone who has ever been frustrated by his or her working relationship with the boss—and who hasn't ever felt this way! Bosses play a critically important role in your career success and getting on the wrong side of this important individual in your working life is not a good thing.

Each of these 100 Ways is designed to illustrate a particular problem that you may encounter when dealing with your boss and then an effective strategy to prevent this problem from reoccurring. You will learn how to deal more effectively with your boss in this fun and practical book filled with invaluable advice that can be utilized every day at work.

Written by Peter R. Garber, the author of *Winning the Rat Race at Work*, this book is a must read for anyone interested in getting ahead. You will want to keep a copy in your top desk drawer for ready reference whenever you find yourself in a challenging predicament at work.

ISBN: 1-895186-98-6   (paperback)
Also available in ebook formats. Order from your local bookseller, Amazon.com, or directly from the publisher at http://www.InTroubleAtWork.com

Want to Get Ahead in Your Career?

Do you find yourself challenged by office politics, bad things happen-ing to good careers, dealing with the "big cheeses" at work, the need for effective networking skills, and keeping good working relation-ships with coworkers and bosses? *Winning the Rat Race at Work* is a unique book that provides you with case studies, interactive exercises, self-assessments, strategies, evaluations, and models for overcoming these workplace challenges. The book illustrates the stages of a career and the career choices that determine your future, empowering you to make positive changes.

Written by Peter R. Garber, the author of *100 Ways to Get on the Wrong Side of Your Boss*, this book is a must read for anyone interested in getting ahead in his or her career. You will want to keep a copy in your top desk drawer for ready reference whenever you find yourself in a challenging predicament at work.

ISBN: 1-895186-68-4   (paperback)
Also available in ebook formats. Order from your local bookseller, Amazon.com, or directly from the publisher at
http://www.mmpubs.com/rats

Your wallet is empty? And you still need to boost your team's performance?

Building team morale is difficult in these tough economic times. Author Kevin Aguanno helps you solve the team morale problem with ideas for team rewards that won't break the bank.

Learn over 100 ways you can reward your project team and individual team members for just a few dollars. Full of innovative (and cheap!) ideas. Even with the best reward ideas, rewards can fall flat if they are not suitable to the person, the organization, the situation, or the magnitude of the accomplishment. Learn the four key factors that will *maximize* the impact of your rewards, and *guarantee* delighted recipients.

101 Ways to Reward Team Members for $20 (or Less!) teaches you how to improve employee morale, improve employee motivation, improve departmental and cross-organizational teaming, maximize the benefits of your rewards and recognition programme, and avoid the common mistakes.

ISBN: 1-895186-04-8   (paperback)
Also available in ebook formats. Order from your local

Corporate Intelligence Awareness: Securing the Competitive Edge

In this compelling new book by a former diplomat, you will learn the secrets (step by step) to developing an intelligence strategy by effective information gathering and analyzing, and then to delivering credible intelligence to senior management. Along the way, you will learn how to better read people and organizations and get them to open up and share information with you—all the while behaving in an ethical, legal manner. Understanding how intelligence is gathered and processed will keep you ahead of the game, protect your secrets, and secure your competitive edge!

ISBN: 1-895186-42-0 (hardcover)
ISBN: 1-895186-43-9 (PDF ebook)

Also available in other ebook formats. Order from your local bookseller, Amazon.com, or directly from the publisher at **http://www.mmpubs.com/cia**

Managing Smaller Projects:
A Practical Approach

So called "small projects" can have potentially alarming consequences if they go wrong, but their control is often left to chance. The solution is to adapt tried and tested project management techniques.

This book provides a low overhead, highly practical way of looking after small projects. It covers all the essential skills: from project start-up, to managing risk, quality and change, through to controlling the project with a simple control system. It cuts through the jargon of project management and provides a framework that is as useful to those lacking formal training, as it is to those who are skilled project managers and want to control smaller projects without the burden of bureaucracy.

Read this best-selling book from the U.K., now making its North American debut. *IEE Engineering Management* praises the book, noting that "Simply put, this book is about helping people control smaller projects in a logical and effective way, and making the process run smoothly, and is indeed a success in achieving that goal."

Available in print format. Order from your local bookseller, Amazon.com, or directly from the publisher at
www.mmpubs.com/msp

 **The Project Management Audio Library**

In a recent CEO survey, the leaders of today's largest corporations identified project management as the top skillset for tomorrow's leaders. In fact, many organizations place their top performers in project management roles to groom them for senior management positions. Project managers represent some of the busiest people around. They are the ones responsible for planning, executing, and controlling most major new business activities.

Expanding upon the successful *Project Management Essentials Library* series of print and electronic books, Multi-Media Publications has launched a new imprint called the *Project Management Audio Library*. Under this new imprint, MMP is publishing audiobooks and recorded seminars focused on professionals who manage individual projects, portfolios of projects, and strategic programmes. The series covers topics including agile project management, risk management, project closeout, interpersonal skills, and other related project management knowledge areas.

This is not going to be just the "same old stuff" on the critical path method, earned value, and resource levelling; rather, the series will have the latest tips and techniques from those who are at the cutting edge of project management research and real-world application.

www.PM-Audiobooks.com

CPSIA information can be obtained
at www.ICGtesting.com
Printed in the USA
FSHW01n1958181018
53136FS